CASTLES

MAN-MADE WONDERS

Jason Cooper

Rourke Enterprises, Inc.
Vero Beach, Florida 32964

PHOTO CREDITS

© James P. Rowan: cover, pages 4, 10, 12, 13, 18;
© Lynn M. Stone: pages 7, 15, 17, 21; © Roger Boyd: title page;
© Frank S. Balthis: page 8

LIBRARY OF CONGRESS
Library of Congress Cataloging-in-Publication Data
Cooper, Jason, 1942-
   Castles / by Jason Cooper.
   p. cm. — (Man made wonders)
   Includes index.
   Summary: Discusses the history, purpose, and construction
of different types of castles.
   ISBN 0-86592-629-8
   1. Castles—Juvenile literature. [1. Castles.]
I. Title. II. Series.
NA7710.C69 1991
728.8'1'094—dc20   91-10940
                         CIP
                         AC

Printed in the USA

TABLE OF CONTENTS

CASTLES

The days of wealthy landowners and their **knights** are gone. But many of their huge, stone castles still stand. Most castles were built between 600 and 1,000 years ago in Europe. The remaining castles tell us much about life in the past.

Castles were used by the landowners, called **nobles,** and kings as both homes and forts. The castles towered over the countryside. They reminded the many people without wealth of the nobles' power.

Hundreds of castles were built in England, Scotland, France, Germany, and other European countries.

Dover, one of England's strongest castles

WHY CASTLES?

Most castles were built during the **Middle Ages.** Europe was divided into small states in those days. Warfare among the little states, or kingdoms, was common.

To help defend their land, kings gave part of it to rich nobles. The nobles built castles and raised armies of private soldiers, their knights.

The knights defended the castles and land around them. They lived with the nobles safely behind the castle's gates and walls.

Rugged stone walls protected castle defenders

EARLY CASTLES

A castle was built where the owner could have a good view of the country. A castle owner also chose a place that would be difficult to attack. Many castles were built on hilltops and along shores of lakes and rivers.

The earliest castles were made of soil and wood. These castles did not stand up well to weather or fire, however. Castle builders soon began to make castles of stone.

Hohenschwangau Castle in the hills of Schwangau, Germany

THE LAST CASTLES

Castles were important in Europe for about 400 years. Then, in the 1400s, castles lost much of their value.

In the 1400s, castles were no longer as safe as they had been. Gunpowder had been invented. Cannon balls, fired by gunpowder, could destroy castle walls.

In addition, kings no longer needed their little armies. They had begun to use one large army. Also, the nobles wanted more comforts than their castles could offer. The comfort of stone castles did not match the castles' grand looks.

Pendennis, one of the last castles (1545), in Cornwall, England

Harlech Castle in Wales, built in the 1200s, was taken by siege in 1458

The Tower of London was a castle for English kings and a prison for their enemies

THE PARTS OF A CASTLE

Many castles had a single, main building called a **keep.** The keep held a great hall, bedrooms, and a little church.

The keep was surrounded by open ground—the castle yard. Beyond the yard was a tall stone wall, or walls. Holes in the walls allowed soldiers to fire arrows out.

Towers and rooms were often part of the walls. Beyond the outer wall was a water-filled ditch known as a **moat.**

Towers were often built into castle walls

BUILDING A CASTLE

A typical castle might take 3,000 workers 20 years to build. Rooms and walls were often added many years later.

Most of the castle was stone. Stone blocks were set together with **mortar,** a mix of sand, lime, and water. (Bolton Castle in England was said to be especially strong because of ox blood in the mortar.)

Castle walls could be 30 feet thick, as wide as a small house. The walls were filled with loose rocks and mortar.

Roofs, beams, floors, and doors were made of wood. Some castle windows were covered by glass.

Crumbling wall of Bolton Castle in Yorkshire, England

LIFE IN A CASTLE

For people who lived in the castle, life there was much like living in a village. The castle met most of their needs. Food and drink were provided by castle bakeries, breweries, and water wells. If it had to, a castle could usually last through a lengthy attack.

Castles were cold and drafty. Paint and cloth wall hangings brightened walls, but they did not warm them. Fireplaces offered some heat. Candles and oil lamps lit the dark rooms.

At Caernarvon Castle in Wales, King Edward I built a town within castle walls

CASTLES TODAY

Hundreds of castles are open to visitors. Hundreds of others have fallen apart or have been destroyed.

Many castles are open to everyone. Countries keep the castles as museums and reminders of life in times long ago. Some castles are owned by families.

A few castles have been carefully repaired. Many of them now look much like they did during the Middle Ages.

The ruins of Richmond Castle in England attract tourists from all over the world

CASTLE ATTACKS

A rugged stone castle was never easy to attack. But castles were attacked with some success, even before cannons.

Attacking armies sometimes climbed over castle walls. They also used huge posts called battering rams to smash through castle gates.

An army could hurl large stones from a **catapult.** The catapult worked like a giant slingshot. Sometimes an attacking army tunneled under the castle's walls.

Glossary

catapult (KAT uh pult) — a machine for hurling such things as large stones

keep (KEEP) — a strong, central part of a castle

knight (NITE) — a special soldier, usually in a noble's private army

Middle Ages (MIH dul A jihz) — European history roughly between the years 500 and 1500

moat (MOTE) — a water-filled ditch around a castle

mortar (MOR ter) — a cementlike mix of lime, sand, and water

noble (NO bul) — an individual in a powerful and wealthy group of landowners

INDEX